W9-BZZ-535

WITHDRAWN
No longer the property of the
Boston Public Library.
Sale of this material benefits the Library

Dysfunctional Families

by Deborah Crisfield

CRESTWOOD HOUSE

New York
Maxwell Macmillan Canada
Toronto
Maxwell Macmillan International
New York   Oxford   Singapore   Sydney

acc 9-8-92 FIELDS CORNER

LIBRARY OF CONGRESS CATALOGING-IN-PUBLICATION DATA

Crisfield, Deborah.
  Dysfunctional families / Deborah Crisfield.—1st ed.
    p.   cm. — (Facts about)
  Includes glossary/index.
  Summary: Defines "dysfunctional family," discussing the problems causing unhealthy behavior in families and possible forms of therapy.
  ISBN 0-89686-722-6
  1. Problem families—United States—Juvenile literature. 2. Problem children—United States—Juvenile literature.   3. Family social work—United States—Juvenile literature. [1. Family problems.]   I. Title.   II. Series: Facts About
HV699.C75   1992
362.82'0973—dc20   91-22088

PHOTO CREDITS
Cover: Jeff Greenberg
Jeff Greenberg: 4, 7, 10, 13, 16, 19, 21, 22-23, 27, 30, 36, 38, 41, 44
Samuel Saylor: 33

Copyright © 1992 by Crestwood House, Macmillan Publishing Company

All rights reserved. No part of this book may be reproduced or transmitted in any form or by any means, electronic or mechanical, including photocopying, recording, or by any information storage and retrieval system, without permission in writing from the Publisher.

CRESTWOOD HOUSE

Crestwood House
Macmillan Publishing Company
866 Third Avenue
New York, NY 10022

Maxwell Macmillan Canada, Inc.
1200 Eglinton Avenue East
Suite 200
Don Mills, Ontario M3C 3N1

Macmillan Publishing Company is part of the Maxwell Communication Group of Companies.

First edition

Printed in the United States of America

10 9 8 7 6 5 4 3 2 1

CONTENTS

WHEN THERE'S A PROBLEM IN THE FAMILY

When he heard his father's car pull into the driveway, Dave raced upstairs to his bedroom. Dave was 14, but he still got scared every time his father came home. His older brother, Mark, had taught him it was best to stay out of his dad's way. Mark had done exactly that. Two years earlier, he'd moved out of the house. He'd never visited and had called only a couple of times since. Dave couldn't wait until he was old enough to leave.

Up in his room, Dave felt safer. He told himself to calm down. Maybe his father would be sober. Sometimes his father just ignored him. He hoped he would today.

"Dave, get down here!" his father yelled. "The lawn looks terrible! Why didn't you mow it?"

"I was going to mow it this weekend," Dave answered, coming down the stairs quickly. He was confused. He always mowed the lawn on the weekend, and his father knew that.

"Can't you see it won't wait until the weekend? It's too long already."

Dave could smell the alcohol on his father's breath. He knew he shouldn't argue. It was never safe to argue

Because their parents' behavior can be so unpredictable, children of dysfunctional families may choose to spend a lot of time alone.

5

with his father when he'd been drinking. But Dave knew he was right this time. "It's Thursday. It always looks this way on Thursdays."

"Don't talk back to me!" His father slapped Dave across the face. "Get out there and do it now."

Dave knew there was no point in arguing. Mowing the lawn now meant he'd miss dinner, but his mom would sneak him some food later. Dave wished she would stand up to his father, but she never did. Sometimes Dave was madder at her than he was at his father. He sighed and headed upstairs to get his sneakers.

His father grabbed him roughly by the arm. "I said get out there now!"

"But I have to get my sneakers," Dave insisted.

"I don't care what you have to get! Do it in your bare feet!" Dave hurried outside.

Dave's father is an alcoholic. He drinks too much and abuses Dave. Dave's mother is too frightened to do anything about it, so she lets the abuse continue. Dave has grown up afraid of his father and resentful of his mother. The older brother, Mark, has left the family entirely. Dave's family is *dysfunctional*.

Many people define a *dysfunctional family* as a family in which the children have to change their behavior in order to cope with a parent's continuing problem. "Functional" means being able to behave or act or work. "Dys" means not normal. So when a family is called dysfunctional, it means that family members are not behaving in a normal manner.

Dysfunction in the family can be caused by a number of things. Alcohol is probably the number one reason for dysfunctional families in the United States. Right now there are about 30 million children whose lives are being turned upside down by an alcoholic in their family.

These children never know what to expect. Will their parent be loving or mean? Will the parent remember to feed them? Will the parent pass out or be sick from too

About 30 million children are affected by an alcoholic in the family.

much drinking? Even something as simple as not knowing when bedtime is can be very confusing for a young child.

Other causes of dysfunction include drug abuse, divorce, death, gambling addiction, mental illness, lack of money, and how the parents themselves were raised. Sometimes a bad method of parenting can be passed down through generations because people don't know how to parent any other way.

How does this happen? How many families are dysfunctional? How can someone tell if his or her family has a problem? How does it affect the children? And, most important, what can be done about it?

DYSFUNCTION IN THE UNITED STATES

When a child is young, he learns by exploring the world around him. He experiments. For instance, a child learns that if he hits his glass of milk, it will spill. He soon learns that he'd rather drink his milk than spill it. In a dysfunctional family, the child may be punished so often that he gets frightened. He is afraid to explore and experiment. He knows that if he makes a mistake, people will get angry.

Often, when there are drugs and alcohol involved, it is worse. The parents are unpredictable. One day the child will be allowed to do something, but the next day she will be punished for it. This can make a child feel frightened, confused, and uncertain.

Many children in dysfunctional families learn that lying is their best defense. They lie to get approval, and they lie to avoid being punished. Lying comes easily to them because it protects them. But it will hurt them later in life.

Dysfunctional families need help to get healthy. Unfortunately, one of the characteristics of a dysfunctional family is *secrecy*. The people in the family don't want anyone else to know that they are having problems. They are too ashamed to get help, and as a result, many children grow up unhappy.

HIDING THE PROBLEM

Six months ago, Beth's father lost his job. He looked for a new one for a while, but no one wanted to hire him. He became more and more depressed, and he started drinking too much. That's when he stopped looking for a new job. Most days he just sits in front of the television and drinks beer.

Dysfunctional families who are willing to talk about their problems have a better chance of becoming healthy.

Beth's mother told her not to worry. She explained that there was nothing wrong with Beth's father—it was just going to take him a little while to get back on his feet. Beth's mom didn't want people to know there was a problem. She kept hoping that her husband would change before anyone found out. She thought she was protecting Beth and the family.

In reality, she only made things worse. It was important that someone talk honestly to Beth about what was going on. At eight, Beth was too young to know how to handle the problem without her mother's help.

When her mother told her that everything was fine, it only confused Beth more. She could see with her own eyes that there was a problem. Sometimes she felt like she must be crazy. Was she imagining the problem? It was easier for Beth to think that she was crazy than to think that her mother was lying to her.

Beth wouldn't talk about it to anyone else either because she didn't want other people to think she was crazy. All this made Beth very lonely and confused.

In Beth's case, her family went from healthy to dysfunctional in a few months. This might not have happened if the family had been willing to face up to the problem.

CONTROL

While all families are different, there are a few traits that children in dysfunctional families have in common. They need acceptance and approval. And they need to feel that they have control. The scariest thing for children is not knowing what's going to happen next.

In a dysfunctional family, children don't know what to expect. Will Mommy leave them all alone in the big house? Will they be yelled at for slamming the door too hard? Will Daddy hit them again?

In order to feel they're in control, these kids blame themselves for the family's problems. If the problems are their fault, then they can do something about them. They can be extra good or stay out of Mommy or Daddy's way. Often, these steps that children take do make a small difference. This just strengthens the children's belief that the problem was their fault to begin with.

Children feel a lack of control if they blame their parents. The bad things can happen at any time, and there is nothing they can do about it. It is also very painful for children to think of their parents as bad. It's much easier for them to think of themselves as bad.

THE HERO

There are different ways of taking control. Sometimes a child tries to take charge of running the family. This type of child is called the *hero*.

Marla's dad left when she was seven. Her mom had a drug problem all her life, but it became worse when Marla's dad left. Her mother became addicted to cocaine. She just stopped caring. Marla had to learn to run the house if she and her younger sister were going to survive. Marla had to be in charge. She made the decisions about how they were going to live.

In the beginning the house was a mess and they ate a lot of toast and cereal. Marla's mom never bothered to

Children of dysfunctional families may avoid making friends because they are embarrassed about their home lives.

make anything and Marla couldn't cook much else. But Marla was a quick learner. She made sure they all had plenty of food and clean clothes. She kept hoping that if their life looked normal, then it would be normal. If her mother noticed how nice their life could be, then she might stop taking the cocaine.

A couple of times Marla hid the cocaine. She hoped her mother might forget about it. But her mother just got angry and hit Marla. Marla didn't hide the cocaine after that. She just tried to make life as easy as possible for the three of them.

It was important to Marla that her family appear problem-free to others. She had already lost her father, and she didn't want anyone to take her away from her sister or her mother. She became very good at lying.

Marla and her sister were careful not to have close friends. They didn't want their mother to do something embarrassing. They didn't want people to see how they lived. But it made them very lonely.

If Marla had let someone get close to her, then she might have gotten help. Someone could have explained to her that her mother was addicted—she couldn't control her need for cocaine. And when she was high, it was hard for her to be a good mother.

Marla knew that it was cocaine that made her mom act this way, but she couldn't understand why her mother would choose the drugs over her children. Even though Marla should have felt good about herself and good about the job she was doing to keep her family life going, she didn't. Her mother never noticed, which just made Marla try harder. Nothing seemed to change her mother, so Marla felt like a failure.

THE SCAPEGOAT

Thirteen-year-old Pete was completely different. He tried to make everything as difficult as possible for his family. It was the only way they noticed him, and it kept them from fighting with each other.

At least once a week, Pete's parents would get into a huge fight. The argument would almost always end with them shouting or hurting each other. Pete hated it all. He soon learned that if he did something bad, his parents would stop fighting and pay attention to him. This way, he had control over his parents' dysfunctional behavior.

Children like Pete are called the *scapegoats*. These children take the focus off their parents' problem. Instead, they are viewed as the problem in the family. If the larger family problem is solved, these children generally stop misbehaving.

THE LOST CHILD

Pete's sister, Michelle, was having problems, too, but nobody knew it. She was a very quiet, very good ten-year-old. She obeyed her parents and all her teachers and never gave anyone any trouble, so people forgot about her. She is what is called a *lost child*.

Michelle didn't have many friends, and she never talked to anyone in her family. She liked to keep to herself, making up stories about normal families. She thought that if she couldn't actually escape from her

family, she could at least escape from them in her mind.

Michelle was often lonely and sad, but she didn't tell anyone. She didn't want to do anything that would get people upset. She learned that complaining only brought trouble. Everything was a lot easier if she just stayed quietly in the background. Michelle figured that if she was careful, no one would get upset.

It may seem that Michelle is dealing with the family better than Pete, but that isn't the case. Pete's anger and fighting let everyone know that he has a problem. It is his way of calling for help. Michelle, on the other hand, will probably be forgotten. However, when she gets older, she may have trouble opening up to people and getting close to them. She could end up leading a very lonely life because no one noticed that she needed help, too.

THE CLOWN

Brian is 30, and he is lonely, too. Even though he is outgoing and lots of people like him, he isn't close to anyone. Anytime someone starts to get serious, Brian turns the conversation into a joke. His way of taking control of a situation is to become a *clown*. Friends have to be around in the bad times as well as the good, and Brian can't handle the bad.

When Brian was young, his mother was addicted to

Children of dysfunctional families may find it hard to discuss their problems with friends.

gambling. She lied to her children, she broke promises all the time, and she often yelled for no reason. Sometimes Brian's mother would stay away from home for days. She even stole money from Brian and his sisters. His home life was awful, but Brian learned he could make it seem better by making everyone laugh.

If a situation became too tense, he would turn it into a joke. The problem couldn't be serious if everyone was laughing. It was Brian's way of taking control. But not every situation can or should be a joke. Brian still avoids problems. Even though he's always laughing and joking, Brian is not very happy. The problems never go away; they are just brushed under the rug.

EATING PROBLEMS

The body is another area where children have control. Some children gain weight. Others lose weight. Some have sex with lots of people. Some get into fights. All these methods are ways children can show themselves and everyone else that they do have control.

Sharon's parents were very strict. Even though she was 15, her parents still treated Sharon as if she were the same age as her two younger sisters. Sharon's parents were very religious. They didn't want Sharon to be tempted by things outside the church. They wouldn't let Sharon go to most movies, and they certainly wouldn't let her date any boys.

18   *Some children make jokes about problems at home to make things seem better.*

When she was younger, Sharon had a lot of friends. But they soon began to drift away. They were all going to parties and Sharon was left out. She felt lonely and different. She hated the fact that her parents weren't like her friends' parents. She couldn't make them understand that they were ruining her life.

Because she had nothing else to do, Sharon put all her energy into running track. Track was one area of her life her parents couldn't control. Sharon was a good runner already, but she decided to be the best runner in the state. She thought that she might even make it to the Olympics if she tried hard enough.

All Sharon's running kept her in good shape, but she wasn't super thin. Her family had big dinners every night, and Sharon was forced to eat everything on her plate. Sharon thought that her running would improve if she lost some weight.

Sharon was pleased when she realized she could make herself throw up after dinner. She loved having this secret from her parents. She liked fooling them. They thought that they could control what she ate, but, in reality, she was the one in control.

Soon it was a problem. Sharon was feeling like she had to throw up after eating anything. Any little bit of food in her body seemed like too much. After lunch in school, Sharon would go straight to the bathroom and stick her finger down her throat. Soon she didn't have to make herself throw up. Her body just wouldn't accept food anymore.

20   *A child with overbearing parents may put all of his or her energy into something that the parents can't control, like sports.*

Her hair and skin looked dull. Her running was getting worse instead of better because she had no energy. Sharon also looked much too thin. No one really paid much attention at first, though. They thought she was thin from so much running. After all, she seemed to be eating big meals.

Finally, Sharon collapsed on the track one day. Her coach rushed her to the hospital. The doctor there said that Sharon was *anorexic*. That meant that she had starved her body. The way she did this was by throwing up. He could tell by her teeth. They were rotting away from all the vomiting she was doing.

Sharon was put on an intravenous feeding tube. The doctor said that she had to get her body used to food again. She would be all right, he thought, because they had caught it in time. Sometimes, though, people with eating problems can die.

Even though Sharon's family didn't seem dysfunctional, it clearly was. Sharon and her family needed to get some help to change.

Parents often miss the signs that their children are anorexic. They see the children doing well in school and succeeding in other areas of life, so they ignore the signs that something might be wrong. Because they see their children every day, they don't really notice how severe the weight loss has been. It often takes someone who hasn't seen the child in a long time to notice the difference.

LOSING A PARENT

Sometimes it is not the parent who is the problem. Sometimes it is the situation. The death of a parent or a divorce will nearly always create a dysfunctional situation for a short period of time.

When Kathryn was ten, her mother died. Everybody told Kathryn that she had to be strong for her father. She was the oldest child. She was going to have new responsibilities, such as cooking and cleaning. And now that her mother was gone, she'd have to look out for her younger brother and sister. Everyone seemed to forget that Kathryn was just a child herself.

Kathryn listened very seriously to all that was expected of her. She tried hard. She had to stop playing with her friends after school, because she always had to be home for her brother and sister. Her grades slipped because there never seemed to be enough time to do all her homework. She had so much to do.

Still, it seemed that her father was never happy anymore. Kathryn remembered what everyone had told her. It was her job to make him feel better. She was failing at her job. Nothing she did seemed to make any difference. Kathryn started thinking that she wasn't very good at anything.

Her father made it even worse by yelling at her for her slipping grades and criticizing her cooking and cleaning. He didn't realize that she was too young to do it all.

Death or divorce can cause a healthy family to become temporarily dysfunctional.

Kathryn didn't realize it either. She just went on thinking that she wasn't good enough.

On top of all this, she was missing her mother as much as her father was. But no one seemed to realize that Kathryn was hurting, too. There was no one who understood, so Kathryn thought that she was wrong to be feeling that way.

When there is a death or divorce in the family, children seem to bounce back, but that's not always the case. The children may be hiding their real feelings in an effort to make things easier. If children get frequent stomachaches or headaches, have sleeping or eating problems, or if their behavior changes radically, then they are sending a signal that they need help.

Death or divorce can be especially tough on the oldest child. This child is often given new responsibilities at a time when it is hard enough just dealing with the old ones. Boys are often told "You're the man of the house now." This puts enormous pressure on these kids. Because most kids want to please their parents, they do their best to fit into their new role in the family. But they are so busy trying to be adults that they end up missing their childhood.

IT'S MY FAULT

Younger children have problems, too. They tend to blame themselves for the divorce or death. They aren't

Very young children have trouble understanding why things go wrong at home. Often they blame themselves.

old enough to understand that some things happen for reasons that have nothing to do with them. They think the world revolves around them.

Three-year-old Amy had a new pair of round-tipped scissors that she wanted to try out. Amy had seen her mom cut flowers from their yard. Amy thought it might be fun to cut some flowers herself. She tried it and it was fun! She spent the morning cutting off the tops of every single flower in the yard.

When Amy's mother found out, she was furious. She

took away Amy's scissors and sent Amy to her room. This was one more problem on top of everything else. She didn't have time to deal with it. She and Amy's father were getting divorced and they were going to have to tell Amy soon. She was not looking forward to it.

The next morning Amy's mother and father called her into the kitchen. Amy's mother had already forgotten all about the flowers. That wasn't nearly as important as telling Amy about the divorce. Amy still remembered about the flowers, though.

When her parents told her about the divorce, Amy thought it was more punishment. First her mom took away her scissors and now she was taking away her daddy. No matter how many times people said it wasn't her fault, Amy was sure it was. Even when she was older and she realized this couldn't be true, she still couldn't get rid of her horrible feelings of guilt.

Amy's reaction is fairly common. Small children usually blame themselves for their parents' divorce. It's even worse when many of the parents' fights have been about the children.

MORE PROBLEMS WITH DIVORCE

Even if a divorce is the best thing for a family in the long run, it is stressful in the short run. And sometimes this situation continues. After a divorce, there is only one parent to look after the children instead of two. So children find themselves left home alone more often. These children are already feeling very upset and insecure because of the divorce. It is difficult for them to be alone at a time when they need extra love and understanding.

When children aren't getting support at home, they look elsewhere. Grandparents and other relatives, teachers, and friends help the most. If a child turns to a caring adult or a responsible group of friends, then it's pretty likely that things will turn out well. But if the child turns to an irresponsible group of friends, then it can be a disaster.

It can be especially difficult if the divorce forces the family to move to a new town. Kids have to make new friends. They are more willing to try drugs and alcohol in order to be accepted. Because they are getting less support and attention from their parents, it becomes very important to have approval from friends.

It is not unusual for children to misbehave after a divorce. They may not realize it, but they want their par-

ents to notice that they need extra help. Children are asking their parents to step in and set the rules for their new family life. It's a tough situation, because this is often the time when a parent is least able to give extra help. And parents themselves aren't sure what the new rules are.

CHILD ABUSE

When a family is dysfunctional because of a death or divorce, the problem usually straightens itself out as the family gets used to its new life. But there are other situations when a dysfunctional family needs outside help in order to heal.

Some parents deliberately hurt their children. This is the most damaging type of dysfunctional family. When a parent deliberately and repeatedly hurts a child, it is called *child abuse*.

Child abuse is a very serious problem in the United States. In 1979, 600,000 child abuse cases were reported. Only ten years later, the number was up to 2,400,000. Some people think that child abuse is on the rise. Others think that it has stayed the same but that more people are reporting it now. Even one case of child abuse is too much.

Child abuse can be emotional, sexual or physical. *Emotional abuse* is when a parent says hurtful things to a child:

"You never do anything right."

"You drive me crazy."

"I hate you."

"You're so stupid."

Statements like these can leave children feeling worthless and unloved. When they hear statements like this over and over, they can't help but think they are true. Parents who say these things are usually blaming the child for things that are wrong in their own lives. They need help to stop. This is true no matter what type of abuse it is.

Sexual abuse occurs when a parent or older person touches a child's genitals in an inappropriate manner or engages in sexual intercourse with a child. The abusers usually know this is wrong, but they cannot stop themselves. They often threaten the children to keep them from telling others. Because of this, most children don't tell anyone. This is the worst thing to do. If the child keeps quiet, the abuse will just continue.

Children need help understanding that whatever happens is not their fault. The abusers need to get help to stop. They need to understand why they do it. A Minnesota study showed that 50 percent of sexual abuse cases involve alcohol. Also, many sexual abusers had been sexually abused when they were children.

Physical abuse is when a parent harms a child's body. Often the child will end up with bruises, cuts, burns, or even broken bones. Many abusers tell themselves that the child needed to be punished. But there is a huge dif-

Four out of five people in prison today were abused when they were children.

ference between a spanking and physical abuse. Many parents do spank their children occasionally. This is not considered abuse. It is when the punishment is more severe and more frequent that it is considered a problem.

AFTER THE ABUSE IS REPORTED

It is very important for abuse to stop. When children are abused, they don't feel good about themselves. As a result, these children usually act in ways that healthy children would not. In fact, four out of five people in prison today were abused as children. If we can stop the abuse early, we may be able to cut down on crime. Most important, when the abuse gets reported, a child can get help. Then the child has a chance to grow up into a healthy adult.

Abuse can be very damaging to a child. Physical abuse can cause serious injury or even death. When the abuse is severe, the child should be put in a *foster home.* A foster home is a temporary place for children to stay until the problems in their family get worked out. This is one way to deal with abuse.

Even though foster homes seem like a good solution, the child doesn't usually see it this way. Instead, the child secs it as a second punishment. First she was beaten and then she was taken from her family. Even though her family might be awful, it is still the only family she knows. It can be very frightening to be taken away from home.

In some instances the child is scnt back to the abusive family. A *social worker* is assigned to talk to the family and watch them to make sure the abuse doesn't happen again. A social worker is someone who is specially trained to deal with family problems. Social workers are paid by the state and are sent in when a problem is discovered.

Unfortunately, even with a social worker, the abuse doesn't always stop. A study in New York City showed that 50 percent of abused children ended up being abused again. But on the good side, that also means that 50 percent of the children and families were helped.

LEARNING HOW TO PARENT

Child abuse is most likely to occur in homes where alcoholism, drug abuse or mental illness exists. But sometimes the child abuse isn't linked with anything else. Some parents aren't prepared for the responsibili-

ties and demands of a child. This is especially true of teenage parents. Some parents just expect too much from their children. When parents are disappointed, it can lead to child abuse.

Two-year-old Jeffrey was being toilet trained. It was very hard for him to learn. He kept forgetting. Every time he went to the bathroom in his pants, his father would hit him. But that just made it worse. Jeffrey became so scared that he couldn't concentrate. He could never remember to use the toilet. Because of this, the beatings got worse. Finally, one beating was so bad that Jeffrey's mother had to take him to the hospital.

Jeffrey's mother told the doctor that Jeffrey had fallen down the stairs. She didn't want anyone to know that Jeffrey's father had hit him like that. She was too embarrassed. But the doctor could tell that she was lying. He finally got her to admit that Jeffrey had been beaten.

A social worker was sent over to Jeffrey's house. She thought it would be okay for Jeffrey to stay with his parents as long as his father could control himself. The social worker talked to Jeffrey's mom and dad. She explained to them that Jeffrey might not be ready to be toilet trained. She also told them that children work much better with praise than with punishment. Praise would make using the toilet something that Jeffrey looked forward to, not something he was frightened of.

The social worker kept in close touch with Jeffrey's family. She answered a lot of questions about how to be a good parent. She left them a number they could call.

Whenever Jeffrey's father felt like hitting Jeffrey, he could call the number and someone would help him find a way to cope with his anger. Jeffrey's family went from being dysfunctional to functional.

Social workers and therapists help families work through their problems. But some parents are too ashamed to get help. Others refuse to admit that a problem exists. If a child isn't brought into a hospital, the abuse may never be discovered.

A family that learns how to cope with dysfunction will have a better home life.

FAMILY THERAPY

Even if it seems that only one person is having trouble, it is a good idea for the whole family to get help. Other family members may be the cause of the problem or they may be making the problem worse without realizing it.

Sometimes one family member isn't willing to get help. For example, if an alcoholic mother won't admit she has a drinking problem, then it's not likely she will seek help to fix the problem. But the rest of the family can and should still get help.

The other family members can learn how to work around the person who has the problem. They can learn how they may be making the problem worse. A counselor can help family members understand how the problem is hurting them and teach them how to cope with it. If the rest of the family is functioning well, it may even benefit the person who has refused to get help.

COUNSELING

Lori's mom had been unhappy for as long as Lori could remember. Lori knew it was her fault. Her mother always said that she wished Lori had never been born. She said that Lori had ruined her life.

In third grade, Lori had a teacher whom she loved. Her name was Ms. Lake. Ms. Lake always took time to praise Lori's work, and she was always telling Lori what a special girl she was. Lori sometimes wished that Ms. Lake could be her mom. One day, Lori told Ms. Lake about the awful things her mother said.

Ms. Lake was very understanding. She thought it might help Lori and her mother to see a *counselor*. A counselor is someone who listens to people's problems and helps them understand why they act the way they do. When people understand why they do bad things, they are less likely to act that way again.

Counselors are similar to social workers. They listen to family problems and try to help solve them. A counselor often has a degree in psychology or psychiatry. Counselors are usually paid by the families that come in for help.

Lori and her mom saw a counselor named Barbara. Barbara helped Lori's mom understand why she was always yelling at her daughter. Lori's mom wasn't very happy with her life. Because she wasn't married and didn't have a good job, she saw herself as a failure. Every time Lori did something wrong, her mother thought of herself. If her daughter was failing, Lori's mom couldn't help thinking she had failed as a mom. That was hard for her to accept. She didn't need any more failure in her life. It was easier to blame Lori.

Barbara helped Lori's mom understand that she wasn't a bad person or a bad mother. She just needed

A counselor can help a family that is having problems.

some help to get her life in order. Once she started feeling better about herself, she was able to get a promotion at her job. She became more satisfied with her life—and less angry at Lori.

Barbara also helped Lori. Lori began to accept the fact that she wasn't a bad person after all. She learned that there were lots of things that she could do well. Before the counseling, Lori and her mom never noticed when Lori did something good. Barbara taught them to pay attention to that.

Counseling is expensive, though. Some families don't have enough money to pay a counselor to help them through the rough times. Social workers, on the other hand, are paid by the government. Social workers offer their services to low-income families at little or no cost. Unfortunately, there are not enough social workers to help all the families that need it.

SUPPORT GROUPS

Another way for families to get help is through *support groups*. Support groups are made up of people who have similar problems. Members teach each other how to cope. The group helps members to feel that they are not alone and that they have someone to talk to who understands. They can help people understand that the problems in their families are not their fault.

For instance, Al-Anon, Alateen and Alatot are support groups that help families with alcohol problems. The members are all people who have had to deal with alcohol problems in their own families. There are 19,000 Al-Anon groups nationwide.

These organizations don't require members to pay any money, and they can be just as helpful as counseling. Support groups can be found for nearly every problem. If there isn't a support group for a particular problem, one can be created very easily. A person can ask counselors, doctors and social workers to find other people with similar problems. Just talking to someone with the same problem can make a world of difference.

HOW DO YOU KNOW?

Some people believe that the dysfunctional label is given to too many families. No family is perfect all the time. Just because a family is going through a rough time does not mean it is dysfunctional. All parents yell at their children sometimes. Many spank their children when they misbehave. And parents don't always have time to listen when a child has a problem. This is normal. Parents make mistakes. A child who has love and understanding most of the time can deal with the times when parents are not perfect.

Dysfunction doesn't have to last forever. Families can work through problems.

The time to worry is when the parents are upset and critical more often than they are loving and supportive. In these cases the dysfunctional behavior is the usual one. Then it's time to get help. A problem can't be solved if no one knows it exists.

FOR MORE INFORMATION

For more information about growing up with an alcoholic parent, contact:

Children of Alcoholics Foundation
P. O. Box 4185
Grand Central Station
New York, NY 10163-4185

or

Alateen/Al-Anon
P. O. Box 862
Midtown Station
New York, NY 10018
(800) 356-9996

These two groups are very willing to help children of dysfunctional families, whether the dysfunction is caused by alcohol or not.

For more information about physical and sexual abuse, contact:

Child Abuse Hot Line
(800) 422-4453

or

Teen Crisis Hot Line
(800) 999-9999

For more information about gambling problems, contact:

Gamblers Anonymous
National Service Office
P.O. Box 17173
Los Angeles, CA 90017
(213) 386-8789

For more information about anorexia or other eating problems, contact:

Anorexia Bulimia Care, Inc.
Box 213
Lincoln Center, MA 01773
(617) 259-9767

GLOSSARY/INDEX

ANOREXIA 23, 46—*A psychologically based eating problem, where a person keeps food from his or her body to the point of starvation.*

CHILD ABUSE 31, 34–35, 37, 38—*When a child is deliberately and repeatedly hurt, either emotionally, physically or sexually.*

CLOWN 17—*A person who attempts to gain control and relieve tension by turning a serious situation into a funny one.*

COUNSELOR 40, 42, 43—*A person who is trained to deal with the problems of a family or an individual. People see a counselor voluntarily and usually pay for the counselor's services.*

DYSFUNCTIONAL 6, 11, 15, 22, 23, 31, 38, 43, 44—*Not working properly.*

DYSFUNCTIONAL FAMILY 6–8, 9, 11, 31, 38, 43, 45—*A family with problems serious enough to force family members to behave in ways they otherwise wouldn't.*

EMOTIONAL ABUSE 31–32—*When hurtful things are repeated regularly so that a person comes to believe them.*

FOSTER HOME 34–35—*A temporary place for children to stay until the problems in their family get worked out.*

HERO 12—*A person who attempts to gain control by taking charge of the family responsibilities.*

LOST CHILD 15—*A person who attempts to gain control by trying to blend into the background and not cause any problems.*

PHYSICAL ABUSE 31, 32, 34, 45—*When a person harms another person's body, by hitting, burning, cutting, et cetera.*

SCAPEGOAT 15—*A person who attempts to gain control by misbehaving in order to shift the attention away from the real problem.*

SECRECY 9—*A trait common in dysfunctional families. Secrecy is used to keep the problem hidden from the rest of the world.*

SEXUAL ABUSE 31, 32, 45—*When a parent or older person touches a child's genitals in an inappropriate manner or engages in sexual intercourse with a child.*

SOCIAL WORKER 35, 37, 38, 40, 42, 43—*A person who is trained to deal with the problems of a family or individual. This person is usually sent to the family by the state because a problem has been discovered.*

SUPPORT GROUP 42–43—*A gathering of people who are all dealing with a similar problem and wish to help others cope with that problem.*